THIS BOOK BELONGS TO

_____

_____

In Praise of
MOTHERS

JARROLD
PUBLISHING

God could not be everywhere and
therefore he made mothers.

Jewish proverb

✳

They say that man is mighty...
But a mightier power and stronger
Man from his throne has hurled,
For the hand that rocks the cradle
Is the hand that rules the world.

William Ross Wallace

✳

All that I am or hope to be,
I owe to my angel mother.

Abraham Lincoln

✳

THE NEST

Sir John Everett Millais 1826–1896

THE READING LESSON

Richard Crafton Green b.1848

I looked on child rearing not
only as a work of love and duty
but as a profession that was
fully as interesting and
challenging as any honourable
profession in the world and
one that demanded the best
that I could bring to it.

Rose Kennedy

✳

A good mother does
not hear the music of the dance
when her children cry.

Proverb

✳

Who ran to help me when I fell,
And would some pretty story tell,
Or kiss the place to make it well?
My Mother.

Ann Taylor

✳

Is not a young mother one
of the sweetest sights life shows us?

William Makepeace Thackeray

✳

A good mother is worth
a hundred schoolmasters.

George Herbert

✳

In Praise of
MOTHERS

JARROLD
PUBLISHING

God could not be everywhere and
therefore he made mothers.

Jewish proverb

⁕

They say that man is mighty...
But a mightier power and stronger
Man from his throne has hurled,
For the hand that rocks the cradle
Is the hand that rules the world.

William Ross Wallace

⁕

All that I am or hope to be,
I owe to my angel mother.

Abraham Lincoln

⁕

THE CENTRE OF ATTRACTION

James Hayllar 1829–1920

Everybody knows that a good mother gives her children a feeling of trust and stability. She is their earth. She is the one they count on for the things that matter most of all.

Katharine Butler Hathaway

✳

A mother's heart
is always with her children.

✳

Making the decision to have a child – it's momentous. It is to decide forever to have your heart go walking around outside your body.

Elizabeth Stone

✳

THE NEW ARRIVAL

Joshua Hargrave Sams Mann fl.1849–1885

Lo! at the couch where infant beauty sleeps,
Her silent watch the mournful mother keeps;
She, while the lovely babe unconscious lies,
Smiles on her slumbering child with pensive eyes.

THE PLEASURES OF HOPE
Thomas Campbell

MOTHERLY LOVE
Gustave-Leonhard de Jonghe
1828–1893

DAUGHTERS OF EVE

Sir Frank Dicksee 1853–1928

*

A woman who can cope with the terrible twos can cope with anything.

Judith Clabes

✳

A mother's love is so strong and unyielding that it usually endures all circumstances…A mother's love perceives no impossibilities.

✳

A mother laughs our laughter,
Sheds our tears,
Returns our love,
Fears our fears,
She lives our joys,
Cares our cares,
And all our hopes and dreams she shares.

Julia Summers

✳

When you are a mother you are never really alone in your thoughts. You are connected to your child and to all those who touch your lives.

✳

A mother always has to think twice,
once for herself and once for her child.

Sophia Loren

✳

Youth fades;
    love droops;
the leaves of friendship fall;
    A mother's secret love outlives them all.

Oliver Wendall Holmes

✳

LUXEMBOURG GARDENS
Albert Edelfelt

MOTHERLY LOVE
Emile Munier b.1810

A mother is not a person to lean on
but a person to make leaning unnecessary.

Dorothy Canfield Fisher

✳

The mother loves her child most divinely, not when she
surrounds him with comfort and anticipates his wants, but
when she resolutely holds him to the highest standards and
is content with nothing less than his best.

Hamilton Wright Mabie

✳

The mother is the most precious possession of the nation,
so precious that society advances its highest well-being
when it protects the functions of the mother.

Ellen Key

✳

I love the modern mother
Who can share in all our joys,
And who understands the problems
Of her growing girls and boys.

❋

Mothers have as powerful an influence over the welfare
of future generations as all other earthly causes combined.

John S.C. Abbott

❋

Any mother could perform the jobs of several
air-traffic controllers with ease.

Lisa Alther

❋

What is a home without a mother?

Alice Hawthorn

❋

PRECIOUS MOMENTS
Edwin Harris 1855–1906

FONDLY GAZING

George Smith

1829–1901

*M*en are what their mothers made them.

Ralph Waldo Emerson

✳

*T*he future destiny of the child
is always the work of the mother.

Napoleon Bonaparte

✳

Womanliness means only motherhood;
All love begins and ends there…

Robert Browning

✳

No one but doctors and mothers know
what it means to have interruptions.

Karl Menninger

✳

I know of no pleasure that quite matches that of seeing your youngster proudly flaunting something you have made.

Ruth Goode

✳

A mother is she who can
take the place of all others but whose
place no one else can take.

Cardinal Mermillod

✳

There isn't a mother
alive who has not lived
in dreaded terror of
'The Empty Nest'.

Erma Bombeck

✳

A GREAT SECRET
Edith Scannell fl.1870–1903

First published in Great Britain in 1996 by
JARROLD PUBLISHING LTD
Whitefriars, Norwich NR3 1TR

Developed and produced by
FOUR SEASONS PUBLISHING LTD
1 Durrington Avenue, London SW20 8NT

Text research by *Pauline Barrett*
Designed in association with *The Bridgewater Book Company*
Edited by *David Notley* and *Peter Bridgewater*
Picture research by *Vanessa Fletcher*
Printed in Dubai

ISBN 0-7117-0865-7

ACKNOWLEDGEMENTS

Four Seasons Publishing Ltd would like to thank all those
who kindly gave permission to reproduce the words and visual
material in this book; copyright holders have been identified
where possible and we apologise for any inadvertent omissions.

We would particularly like to thank the following
for the use of pictures: *Bridgeman Art Library, e.t. archive,*
Fine Art Photographic Library.

Front Cover: SLEEP, *Henry Nelson O'Neil*
Title Page: GOLDEN HOURS, *Hans Tichy 1861–1925*
Frontispiece: MOTHER'S LITTLE HELPER, *George Goodwin Kilburne 1839–1924*
Back Cover: MOTHERLY LOVE, *Emile Munier b.1810*